CW00925457

# AN ENGLISH FIGURE
Two Essays on the Work of John Michell

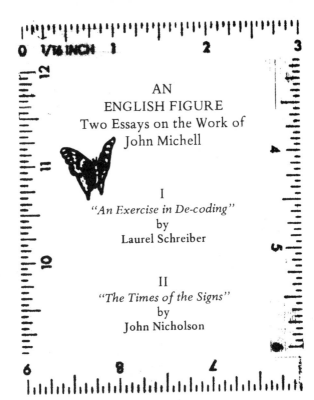

# AN
# ENGLISH FIGURE
Two Essays on the Work of
John Michell

I
*"An Exercise in De-coding"*
by
Laurel Schreiber

II
*"The Times of the Signs"*
by
John Nicholson

BOZO
1987

Bozo's Educational Aids • Number One

AN ENGLISH FIGURE
Two Essays on the work of John Michell

February 1987
© BOZO

ISBN 0 904063 19 4

## Acknowledgements

Our thanks to Paul Sieveking for proof-reading and paste-up; Bridget Tisdall for additional lay-out; Anthony Roberts for help with the Bibliography; Dedwydd Jones for reading the manuscript; Cecilia Boggis for typesetting; and John Michell for long sufferance. The book was designed by Zero Speed. Special thanks to John Michell for permission to reproduce the paintings by Maxwell Armfield.

**BOZO**

*[full address]*
BM BOZO
LONDON WC1N 3XX
ENGLAND

Cover printed by Kall-Kwik, Bedford
Printing by I.P. West One, 12 Heddon Street, London W1
Binding by Panther Press, Bedford

# Contents

# Illustrations

*Cover photograph of John Michell by Evelyn Honig*

# THE EVIDENCE
## Twenty-one years of publishing

[In this Bibliography a ★ indicates the first edition of a book]

## 1967
★ *The Flying Saucer Vision;* **Sidgwick & Jackson.**

## 1969
*Glastonbury, A Study in Patterns* (contributor); **RILKO.**
★ *The View Over Atlantis;* Sago (distributed by Garnstone).
*The Ley Hunter* magazine, revived (contributor and inspiration); **Paul Screeton.**
Contributor; Findhorn Trust anthology.

## 1970
Introduction to *The Old Straight Track* by Alfred Watkins (1925); Garnstone.

## 1971
*Britain, A Study in Patterns* (contributor); **RILKO.**
★ *City of Revelation;* Garnstone.

## 1972
*The View Over Atlantis* (revised); **Garnstone.**
*A Defence of Sacred Measures* [Radical Traditionalist Papers No.1]; Cokaygne.
*The New Jerusalem at Glastonbury* (included in Zodiac House's Glastonbury anthology, 1976); **Zodiac House.**

## 1973
*The Fall of Babylon* [Radical Traditionalist Papers No.2]; dual language edition; Cokaygne.
*A Defence of People and Population* [Radical Traditionalist Papers No.3]; Cokaygne.
*A Little History of Bladud;* West Country Editions.
★ *The Old Stones of Land's End* (subscription edition); Elephant.
*Bladud of Bath, the British King Who Tried to Fly,* by Howard C. Levis (1919); (republished); West Country Editions.

*Souvenir Programme for the Official Lynching of Michael Abdul Malik* (compiled with William Levy); **Cokaygne.**

Introduction to *Feng Shui* by E.J. Eitel; (reprint of 1873 edition); **Cokaygne.**

*The Propaganda of the Metric System* by Edward Nicholson (1912); republished; **Radical Traditionalists.**

*The View Over Atlantis* (paperback of 1972 edition); **Abacus.**

*The City of Revelation* (paperback of 1971 edition); **Abacus.**

## 1974

*The Flying Saucer Vision* (paperback of 1967 edition); **Abacus.**

Introduction to *The Old Straight Track* (paperback of 1970 edition); **Abacus.**

*The Old Stones of Land's End;* (public edition of 1973 edition); **Garnstone.**

Introduction to *Standing Stones of Maeshowe* by Magnus Spence (1894); **RILKO.**

Introduction and editorial amendments to *The Canon* by William Stirling (1897); **RILKO/Garnstone.**

## 1975

*The Fanatic* magazine No.1 (editor); **The Author.**

*The View Over Atlantis;* (new edition). **Abacus.**

★ *The Earth Spirit, its Ways, Shrines and Mysteries;* **Thames & Hudson.**

*Just Measure* magazine No.1; (editor); **Anti-Metrication Board.**

*Souvenir Programme of the Anti-Metric Garden Fete;* (instigator); **Anti Metrication Board.**

## 1976

Introduction to *Mother Shipton* by Anon (1916); (withdrawn); **West Country Editions.**

*The Fanatic* magazine No.3; (co-editor); **The contributors.**

*Just Measure* magazine No.2; (editor); **Anti-Metrication Board.**

*The Hip Pocket Hitler;* (compiler); **Hassle Free.**

*Un Autre Monde;* (editor); magazine to accompany Michell's series of talks to the Lindisfarne Association, New York; **the Author.**

## 1977

★ *A Little History of Astro-Archaeology;* **Thames & Hudson.**
★ *A Short Life at the Land's End, J.T. Blight FSA, Artist, Penzance;* by **subscription.**
★ *Phenomena, a Book of Wonders* (with R.J.M. Rickard); **Thames & Hudson**
*Just Measure* magazine No.3; (editor); **Anti-Metrication Board.**
*To Represent Our Saviour as That Great Cock is not Blasphemy;* [Radical Traditionalist Papers No.4] ; **Open Head.**

## 1978

*Just Measure* magazine No.4; (editor); **Anti-Metrication Board.**
Revised article in the new edition *Glastonbury* anthology first published 1976 by Zodiac House; **Rider.**

## 1979

*Just Measure* magazine No.5; (editor); **Anti-Metrication Board.**
★ *Simulacra, with 196 illustrations of Faces and Figures in Nature;* **Thames & Hudson.**
Introduction to *Inventorum Natura* by Pliny the Elder; illustrated by Una Woodruff; **Paper Tiger.**
*Old Stones of Land's End;* (third edition); **Pentacle.**
Introduction to *Feng Shui;* (second edition of 1973 reprint); **Pentacle.**
*The House of Lords UFO Debate;* (introduction and commentary); **Pentacle & Open Head.**

## 1980

*Schumacher Lectures;* (contributor); **Blond and Briggs.**

## 1981

★ *Ancient Metrology;* **Pentacle.**
Introduction and editorial amendments to *The Canon* by W. Stirling (1897); paperback (revised edition); **RILKO & Thorsons.**

## 1982

* *Megalithomania;* **Thames & Hudson.**
* *Living Wonders, Mysteries and Curiosities of the Animal World* (with R.J.M. Rickard); **Thames & Hudson.**
  *The Concordance of High Monarchists of Ireland* [Radical Traditionalist Papers No.5]; **The Author.**

## 1983

* *The New View Over Atlantis;* **Thames & Hudson.**
  Introduction to *The Pallinghurst Barrow* by Grant Allen (1892); **The Author.**

## 1984

* *Eccentric Lives and Peculiar Notions;* **Thames & Hudson.**
  Revised introduction to *Feng Shui;* (third edition of 1973 reprint); **Synergetic.**
  Introduction to *3 Stories by George Gissing;* **The Author & Richard Adams.**

## 1985

  *Stonehenge, Its Druids, Custodians, Festivals and Future* [Radical Traditionalist Papers No.6]; **The Author.**
  Introduction to *Lost Lyonesse* by Beckles Wilson (1902); [Pocket Pals Series]; **AdCo.**

## 1986

  *Stonehenge, Its History, Meaning, Festival, Unlawful Management, Police Riot '85 and Future Prospects;* (new edition of Radical Traditionalist Paper No.6); **The Author.**
  Introduction to *The Life, Hymns and Work of Proclus;* **Phanes (USA).**
  *Chernobyl and the Time After;* (contributor); **Dianus Trikont (Munich).**

## 1987

* *The Dimensions of Paradise;* **Thames & Hudson.**
* *A Traveller's Key to Sacred England;* **Knopf (USA).**

## UNPUBLISHED WORKS
★ *Euphonics, a Poet's Dictionary of Sounds;* illustrated by Merrily Harpur.
● *The Bed-Sitting Room Anthology* (compiler).
★ *A Fool's Guide to World History* (fragments).

## ARTICLES & ESSAYS
John Michell has contributed to many periodicals, not only in Britain. This list is not exhaustive. Further details can be found in a pioneering study of Michell scholarship by Paul Screeton (editor *The Ley Hunter* 1969-1976) which appeared in *Stonehenge Viewpoint;* July-August 1982.

| | |
|---|---|
| *Albion* | *New Life* |
| *Arcana* | *New Musical Express* |
| *Bres* | *New Seed* |
| *Co-Evolution Quarterly* | *The New Statesman* |
| *Dorset Country Life* | *New World Journal* |
| *Ealing First Year Graphics* | *Pendragon* |
| *East West Journal* | *Quicksilver Messenger* |
| *The Fanatic* | *Radionic Quarterly* |
| *The Field* | *Resurgence* |
| *Fortean Times* | *Second Look* |
| *The Fred* | *The Shaman* |
| *Frendz* | *The Spectator* |
| *Gandalf's Garden* | *Stonehenge Viewpoint* |
| *High Times* | *Temenos* |
| *History Makers* | *The Times* |
| *Image* | *Torc* |
| *International Times* | *Undercurrents* |
| *Journal of Geomancy* | *Vogue* |
| *The Ley Hunter* | *Wiltshire Folklife* |
| *The Listener* | *etc.* |
| *Nature* | |

The publishers welcome additions or corrections which may be included in future editions.

# AN EXERCISE IN DE-CODING
*Laurel Schreiber*

Knowing my addiction to books and to the odd, my sister-in-law was delighted when her Book Club solved the problem of what to give me for Christmas. So much was a happy coincidence. Her pleasure was dashed when the book arrived. Here was the unfortunate coincidence. As it was by one of my favourite authors, she was sure that I would have already bought a copy. However, as I had been unable to afford the full-price edition — the reverse coincidence — everything turned out for the best.

During the festivities I took the book in small doses. This was easy because it was in the form of short, self-contained 'chapters', each one a separate topic. The unifying subject was correctly described by the title *Eccentric Lives and Peculiar Notions*. The good Book Club members get their money's worth, for the author paraded notable examples of both types, most of them not familiar to collectors of oddities. Here were cranks and nuts to satisfy any palate.

But was that all? The first hint that there was more to this book than another freak show ought to have been clear to any discerning reader, for the author, John Michell, was credited on the sleeve with a substantial body of work, principally about the philosophy of the ancients as manifested in our landscapes and sites. Why should such an author pose as a pecuniary showman of freaks?

Or is it a freak show? Certainly there are a number of eccentrics in the Sitwell tradition, but rather off-key. There are as many examples of crank theorists. So the book is a blend of two genres, and satisfies both.

There is trickery. We are swallowing ideas in disguise. Indeed, this device has been so successful that it has satisfied the vulgar. Because it has fooled the Book Club, it has reached them in enormous numbers!

Examine the book more closely. A major criticism has been the lack of a guide in the form of an Introduction and Conclusion. This pattern seems consistent as there is no editorialising comment about the various specimens. The readers are free to make up their own minds. Naturally this is an onerous task, beyond those who are accustomed to having their thinking done for them. Yet it is precisely this absence of warning signals which has made the book slip effortlessly onto the Book Club list. It looks harmless. That is its confidence trick — before you read it.

Yet there is more going on. Every writer faces the quandary of whether to step aside or to be consciously present in the book. The Victorians rhetorically addressed their Gentle Readers. The writer as performer was epitomised by Dickens doing his own 'Readings from Dickens' show. Another standard device has been to present the work as a 'discovered' manuscript, or simply to remove one's name altogether. Since we are currently wooed by new crazes, such as 'semiotic novels', it is reasonable to expect a few people might be aware of such traditional considerations.

As the author has not turned up we jump straight in and find two things immediately. Firstly the writing is elegant, secondly there are wild jokes. One starts the book: "The woodcock is hard to shoot because of its zig-zag flight, and Mr John Rutter Carden of Barnane Castle, Tipperary, was generally known as Woodcock Carden because he also seemed impervious to gunshot." Other features add to the witty tone: the obscure knowledge; the interesting fact about odd attributes in Nature; the strange name and affectionate nickname; and the dry, cliff-hanging, ending. But most of all it is the ability to mix together seemingly unconnected and unpromising material which warns us to watch the conjuror's hands.

After this opening flourish we are immediately treated to another display of hilarious behaviour, made more delightful by the light touch in the telling. (And they complain there is no editorialising?) The Irish Question becomes a village comedy. In case this should enrage the worthy, though humourless, causists it is shown that this urbane view was shared by the people involved, who admired their landlord not only for dodging their bullets but for his high spirits.

For Mr Carden fell in love. Hopelessly, blindly and eternally. Nothing odd about that, nor reprehensible. Indeed for centuries we have been told this is an enviable condition. Cupid's arrow hit the man who was bullet-proof. But Mr Carden's love was based on a false premise: the object of his passion was quite indifferent to him and had never given him encouragement. His love was of the ideal sort which mocked his name: he was no rutting creature although his desire trapped him in a rut.

Yet, such is the power of a true obsession, all the proofs of a mistake only reinforce the determination

15.

and conviction. So splendid was the transparently false passion expressed by Mr Carden that he offered the classic spectacle of a fool. So admirable and unfounded was his devotion that the public could enjoy the quality, as it were distilled, in its purest form. When Mr Carden attempted forcible abduction, bungled it, and provided a wonderful chase scene — he became a hero.

The story ended on the same note. Mr Carden never wavered in his faith, and his benign condition shed its blessings on all who surrounded him in the form of remarkable hospitality. The persecuted lady was less fortunate, though she seems to have found some consolations. The affair provided excellent material for conversion into legend through song. Of such stuff was Don Quixote made.

In this first chapter the book's approach is plainly laid out. By using a commonly understood condition the readers have been introduced to the world of paradox. For this is an example of a belief system which, due to a misconception, turns convention on its head. Many comedies and tragedies have been built on such misunderstandings. Isn't *King Lear* triggered by such a trivial mistake? The comic novels of Thomas Berger thrive on this sort of cross-purpose.

But to apply this process back on itself is to query the very possibility of belief! In a celebration of Charles Fort, the arch priest of oddities, Michell wrote: "The real heretic, against whom every other school joins ranks, is the one who questions the very nature of belief." (*Fortean Times* 41.)

The second chapter moves even further and faster.

It introduces us to a couple who had also been local characters, but known to the author. Therefore there is an immediate charm in this generous gesture to people who would otherwise have been dismissed.

This chapter is also remarkable for plunging us immediately into the actual experience of how belief originates. We cannot know why Mr Carden decided on his obsession but we learn how this couple had their belief confirmed and strengthened by a strange occurrence. Of course the episode is fair game: to the psychiatrists it is a clinical case history; to the mystics it is a visionary experience. So the commentators hold contradictory beliefs, which therefore cancel out each other and return us to the original point: what is the nature of belief? Who holds the valid belief — the psychiatrist, the mystic, or the old couple? "All such beliefs and theories have one feature in common: they cannot be verified." (*Simulacra*, Thames and Hudson, 1979.) Should we therefore reject them all? If we can disbelieve them all, simultaneously, why should we not simultaneously believe them all? Or rather than believing them all, can we not simply accept them all, since they clearly exist? Is this what is meant by "fourfold vision"?

By choosing a couple whose devotion had sustained them for their long lives, the author offers an example of a love which is real, unlike Mr Carden's. This choice also conveniently leads us from a belief based on emotions to one based on intellect, the head not the heart. Mr Carden's belief was peculiar to him but this couple share the same belief. So we see how an impossible, or freak, belief can be held by more than one person. By implication this reminds us of the other cultic beliefs foisted on Glastonbury. For this old couple were regulars on the Glastonbury landscape.

Mention of this place instantly evokes a multitude of impressions but, by concentrating on one peripheral couple's belief system, the author is able to hold up another allegory — this time for the entire complex of beliefs attributed to Glastonbury and everything it symbolises. All the fanatics and bigots are delicately defused by this gentle story of an ordinary, poor, simple, kind-hearted old couple who spent their lives in the service of their belief. In a way they come across as members of a pious Order, consisting only of themselves. Once more we see how their absolute conviction sustained them.

How do such people manage in the unreal world? The answer is that this is a question which only occurs to us, never to them. True believers do not see the world in terms of material success or failure, but only in relation to their belief. Is this not true of us when we ask that question?

This is not an original observation, for it applies to every belief, whether religious, atheistical, scientific, political or pathological. Which is precisely the point. By showing us that there is no difference in the process of belief — whether held by mad lovers, crazy mystics, or current orthodoxy — the book ironically and humorously raises immense possibilities. By describing unconventional behaviour and beliefs the author gives us a chance to re-examine conventional wisdom.

Some years ago, in an idiosyncratic magazine

dedicated to restoring the language of prophecy, Michell described the 'choice' facing the believer. "Those who take God seriously and are prepared to listen to this nonsense must also be prepared to take the consequences, which, on His own word emphatically repeated throughout the Scriptures, are unlikely to be *materially advantageous*." No true believer understands the material world so the accusation that only the wealthy can afford eccentricity is shown to be silly. (That may be true of the eccentric collections.) The poor are just as mad. Money has nothing to do with it — some of these examples do everything that ought to lead to ruin, only to end up with more riches. The opposite is more frequently true, but either way is irrelevant. "It is perfectly ridiculous to kill yourself just because people laugh, and whoever does so is victim of a stupid moralistic approach to life with *popular approval* as its highest aspiration. If God tells you to give away all your possessions and go and eat grass, you can either do so or not . . . So if you are fortunate enough to be chosen by God for some desperate act and gullible enough to listen, it only remains to enjoy the high delights (often experienced in retrospect) or the harassed existence and such consolation as may be obtained from 'Blessed are the poor in spirit for theirs is the Kingdom of Heaven'."

The resonances should now be easier to trace, though there are many, many concealed delights and dangers. In case this sounds as if I am offering a guide-book when the author offers none, I rush to deny this suggestion. No essay can ever improve on the original! But it does offer one reader the chance to express her enjoyment and to hope others will also play the game. Like the decoders of the universe, they can never improve on the original but may, by their efforts, afford themselves some pleasant fancies.

After the Glastonbury couple's fixation on explaining everything in terms of King Arthur, we meet the 'Loyalists of the Flat Earth'. This is such a standard crankery that readers can safely enjoy the knockabout as various attempts are made to 'prove' the belief. Except that the next chapter turns the flat earth inside out to offer other believers, equally sincere, who know that the earth is round. And hollow. And we are living *inside*.

So the japes continue. In the same way that we were focussed on the old couple to comment obliquely on Glastonbury-type beliefs, so we are told about a Catholic priest who spent his life fighting to expose usury. Rather than engaging the banks he found himself in conflict with the Pope! Once more the subtle use of metaphor casts an eccentric light on a 'burning' issue which has been agonised over endlessly and lethally.

For this is another characteristic of the book. It is quirky. In its zig-zag way it deals with the deepest subjects but in the lightest manner. This is not to suggest triviality or archness. On the contrary the dry humour and elegant style are safeguards against any such slovenliness or indulgence. This is a very stylish number!

Where else could you find the supreme expression of literature used as a parlour game? In fact this is another clue. As the works of Shakespeare are of no literary interest but provide the padding to conceal the real message, so the famous words are an elaborate secret language. They will only reveal their true meaning when rearranged by an initiate who knows the correct combination of anagrams, acrostics, crosswords, codes . . . A key is needed to unlock every code, or intelligence, or invocation. It is the device which opens secrets, whether of man or the cosmos.

So this book is like the instructions leaflet for an invisible game. All done with mirrors. I have only touched on the first five chapters and there are seventeen more to enjoy. I shall not spoil it further. Indeed, my only excuse for 'explaining' is that this essay is *my* way of playing the game. Remember, I was given the book at a time of party games. Seen in this way each 'chapter' or episode, is a metaphor. These combine to form an enormous allegory in the manner of Breughel's illustrated *Proverbs,* or Hogarth's medley *Cruelty, Superstition and Fanaticism.*

So is belief necessarily exclusive?

"The universe is in effect a crank's charter in that it will obligingly reflect back to the theorist any ideas projected onto it." (*Simulacra.*) Well, that could also apply to this book. Or, to go to the next Chinese box inside: three of the chapters show how people have applied such an approach to Shakespeare's works. If the reader begins to reel, that is nothing to worry about either. Shakespeare, this book, or the universe — anything — can be chosen for such games, like a multidimensional puzzle.

Rather than imposing theories onto the world, native cultures delighted in receiving messages — or patterns — from the world. This was also true of the classical world. "The ancients, said Socrates, were uncomplicated, and if a certain rock was known for telling the truth, they would listen to it." (*Simulacra.*) Aristotle considered the highest ability of poetry was to see the like in the unlike. Therefore this ability, or process, which recognizes patterns, amounts to a perception of the unity of all things.

If this ability is intrinsic to the world, and therefore to our perception, it follows that it is still available. It has been consciously suppressed by society with consequences that are increasingly apparent. Occasionally it breaks out, however, in eccentric lives and peculiar notions which society, rapidly and ruthlessly, attacks. People are suprised to learn how recent is the Conventional Belief System with its central belief that there ought to be only one way of looking at things, and only one reality. Truth is much kinder.

By showing the workings of this process in terms of recognisable human behaviour, Michell has offered another peculiar way into the great mysteries. In his other works his 'cover story' used different sorts of measurable and tangible phenomena, from megaliths to flying saucers, from Platonic number to unacknowledged species. In *Eccentric Lives and Peculiar Notions* his examples are people themselves, the ultimate living wonders. (Doubtless he will now be deluged with stories of everybody's favourite 'incredible loony'. Perhaps it will make a pleasant change from being the target for every computer mathematician or spotter of winged feet. That is the price for making something clear: everybody offers you their proofs.)

So this book belongs at the heart of Michell's work. If there had been any doubt, surely a glance at the choice of subject ought to have given away the game. Here are many of the author's old favourites: the notion of evolution; of an ancient, canonical tradition; of ways to increase enlightenment; of great secrets in code ... and, transcending them all, the hope of achieving harmonious behaviour. In *Simulacra* we were shown how likenesses of the Creator could be spotted in His work: even faces of Christ have been 'proved' in loaves, trees, clouds, etc. In much the same way the author is everywhere in this book, if you keep your eyes open. Apart from his beloved hobbyhorses here are his friends and acquaintances, here he is in person visiting cultic communities in Europe and America. It is almost a mocking self-portrait (Glastonbury, Atlantis, Druids, the New Jerusalem mystical and literal, conspiracies in History and Literature ... ) but, again, he stands aside, always politely amused. In the midst of all this whirling craziness the conjuror retains his balance with style. Even the biography on the dust-jacket is mischevious — Eton, naval intelligence — are we meant to take this seriously? Is he another defector? Is it all a triple bluff? Why should we believe any of it? It doesn't add up. No previous work by John Michell has allowed a picture of the author — here we are to accept The Author in classic pose, complete with bow tie and huge cigar, laughing at some joke! What proof have we that the publishers aren't fooling?

Am I completely deluded in reading all these subtleties into the book? Maybe I have imagined it all and have projected my own obsessions onto a plain tale of idiots. Is there nothing here but the usual aimless concoction, randomly hacked out in the dungeons of Thames and Hudson and put out under the name of one of their captive starving writers, who would do anything for money and fame? You are free to decide for yourself by the simple act of buying your own copy and seeing what it means to you. Or, if you prefer, you can play Consequences.

*Opposite: A rock face or simulacrum*

In John Nicholson's essay the discussion of a title is indicated by its heading at the top of the page — while the start of its section is indicated in the text by the title in **bold type**.

# THE TIMES OF THE SIGNS
## *John Nicholson*

Why John Michell? According to *East West Journal*, June 1985: "Within the Earth Mysteries field, which is growing in proponents and influence, Michell is a venerable father figure. Outside this still small cadre of geomancers, dowsers, Druids and new Atlanteans, the name of John Michell isn't too well known yet." There has been a handful of commentaries on the man and his work which portray him as a fool or genius. Yet both opinions claim him as the seminal figure. Michell has been publishing his ideas for 20 years in over a dozen books and many essays and articles, so it is possible to form a picture of his message.

Two things are immediately striking. Firstly, how Michell has introduced a new range of subjects and, secondly, how his work has transformed attitudes to the Occult and to Science.

In the interview mentioned above Michell refers to his role as an agent of transformation in terms easily recognisable to an American readership. He likens himself to "a cosmological switchman" who is hunting "just one right switch to effect an immediate revolution in cosmology".

By his own account John Michell came late to books. His first work *The Flying Saucer Vision* was published in 1967 when he was thirty-five. This is an unusual pattern as writers rarely arrive fully grown.

According to another interview[1] Michell was reduced to writing when his inheritance was exhausted by high living. He also blames "business inefficiency", a polite description for "an addiction to con-men". All that remained were the pleasures of speculative contemplation. It was a fate he has not regretted. In the Preface to *The New View Over Atlantis* (1983) he observes, "No form of study can be more delightful and beneficial than this one, for in pondering the designs and works of the ancient sages one is exposed to the noble mentalities of our kind, which these works reflect".

The stoicism gives an indication of Michell's background and the sort of life he would have been expected to lead. Educated at Eton and Trinity College, Cambridge, he came down in the early 1950s when London was still a hard-playing city. From reminiscences we catch glimpses of a young blood revelling about town, with a taste for the pleasures of the Arts. For a spell he painted, exhibited, and worked in a gallery. Other jobs included estate agency, which would have given an insight into the values set on property. Michell's national service had taken him to naval intelligence as a Russian interpreter. By the end of the 1950s he had become a regular on the Notting Hill Gate 'scene' which has become famous thanks to Colin McInnes: the sharp youngsters, the mix of black and white, the high spirits and high drugs, the dreams of better worlds . . .

Michell's first book, The Flying Saucer Vision, dealt with the idea of a cosmological switch brought about by an agency, in this case flying saucers. The appearance of UFOs, like the Atom Bomb, was seen by the late 1950s as proof of the New Epoch. Within 20 years a new lore had grown to such proportions that the eminent psychologist Jung made an analysis of 'A modern myth of things seen in the skies'. *The Flying Saucer Vision* takes Jung's remarkable essay as its starting point and Michell's second book, *The View Over Atlantis*, is prefaced by a reference to it. As it is possible to see Michell's work as an attempt to find answers to the questions raised by Jung it is worth examining them.

Jung saw UFOs as a further confirmation of his theory of archetypes, ie that there is a number of basic patterns or images in human experience which find their expression or manifestation in all ages and cultures. Jung called these archetypes 'psychic dominants' instead of the name they used to have: gods. Jung was fighting a battle in which the odds were already stacked. Due to the pressure of orthodoxy it was more acceptable to believe in UFOs than in divinities. With UFOs the need to transcend, which is the basis of religious experience, had been transposed into a semi-scientific atmosphere. UFOs were thus acceptable to those who scorned mysticism. Devotees could believe in the notion of human beings taken away by aliens in space craft but would ridicule the possibility that a superhuman or divine entity might spirit away men and women.

Underneath Jung's rhetoric lay the fight between the traditional, religious, approach and the proselytising new faith in Science and Reason, still confident that the Atomic Age would be the promised utopia. UFOs were a good test case because, according to Jung, "the reasonable opinion of the majority" regarded belief in UFOs as a sort of collective madness. Therefore UFOs offered the chance to show how a superstition, a myth, a false belief system, originated. In turn this could reveal the false basis on which all religion rests. UFOs could be used as a metaphor to show how and why people believe in the divine or the ineffable. The supernatural had already been reduced to the realm of madness and now the new superior wisdom, Psychology, would at last be able to bring about "long-lasting transformations of the collective psyche".

It is interesting to see how psychologists were to be the agents of transformation instead of the UFOs. For psychologists, like UFOs and the other 'signs', agreed there was an urgent need for a new order. As Michell put it[2], "The changed conditions, which we are already beginning to face, will necessitate a reassessment of the fundamentals of every branch of science and knowledge. There is urgent work to be done in every field."

According to Jung, "In the individual such phenomena as abnormal convictions, visions, illusions, etc only occur where there is a split between the conscious attitude and the unconscious contents opposed to it. Precisely because the conscious mind does not know about them and is therefore confronted with a situation from which there seems to be no way out, these strange contents cannot be integrated directly, but seek to express themselves indirectly, thus giving rise to unexpected and apparently inexplicable opinions, beliefs, illusions, visions and so forth." Jung transferred this idea, as a principle, to the external or real world. "Any unusual natural occurrences such as meteors, comets, 'rains of blood', a calf with two heads, and such like abortions are interpreted as menacing omens, or else signs are seen in the heavens."

For Michell "The reappearance of flying saucers and our reawakening interest in extra-terrestrial life represents a return to an orthodoxy temporarily abandoned." This turns Jung upside-down. For Jung "inexplicable opinions, beliefs, illusions or visions" should be seen as signs of "psychic disturbance" in the same way that the supernatural is not only a form of madness but a *projection* of madness. Jung does not deny such things occur nor that they are 'natural'. What his philosophy requires is a break in the causal claim which traditionally links such phenomena to a divine or external agency. Consequently we are asked to make an even greater leap of faith. "Things can be seen by many people independently of one another, or even simultaneously, which are not physically real." Psychology wants it both ways: the "strange contents" are real and unreal, they exist and don't exist.

Whatever the cause there were irrefutable signs that a transformation in outlook was taking place in the mid 1960s. One measure of the scale of this psychic disturbance is the resentment it still generates.

Michell also saw UFOs as a metaphor and suggested they were "a distant threat to the established order", and they "put us in a state of mental anarchy" which is a preliminary to the new age. He explored the symbol of an opportune intervention by external forces — whether as UFOs, mind-transforming drugs, or drilling a hole in one's skull. All were ways of causing a colossal shock, of completely changing perception. The realisation had grown that initiatory rites had made use of similar techniques to traumatise those who sought greater wisdom. Huxley had explored the idea of hallucinatory drugs as a way of opening 'the doors of perception' and by the mid 1960s thousands were taking trips across this threshold. Some never came back and those who did brought tales of such wonder or horror that their lives could never be the same. Like people who saw UFOs these 'heads' had indelible experiences. They told of strange lights, colours and sounds. They spoke of alien senses such as being able to read minds by touch or just by a person's 'vibrations'. Their sense of awareness was so intense they felt they were experiencing the universe.

Were these drugs able to transform the psyche in some biological way? Could they cause Man to evolve to another form of intelligence? As those who experienced UFOs began to see with the 'flying saucer vision' so these drugs which affected the psyche produced a psychedelic consciousness. There was an urgency to spread the gospel to save the world. In this messianic mission everything was done to 'turn you on' to the new perspective. The inner effects were recreated externally with light shows to increase the sounds of the 'head' music. Posters were printed in festering dayglo which seemed to hover off the paper, or became 3-dimensional under 'black lite'. Lettering swirled so wildly it could only be deciphered by initiates. It was like some vast anamorphic game with hidden pictures which only come to life when viewed with a reflecting device (a magic mirror) to transform the distorted designs into delightful full colour scenes. In order to share in these amazing new secrets more and more people 'blew their minds', either with the help of hallucinogens or simply by ignoring their conditioning and 'dropping out'. Around the world the new contactees numbered millions.

Enormous amounts of imaginative energy were poured into creating the new music. In turn it energised a generation. An example of the mixture was the Jimi Hendrix Experience which was so steeped in the imagery of UFOs and other worlds that there was a popular legend that as Hendrix played UFOs were sighted hovering over the stage and aiding him to perform their freaked-out music. That another cult, drugs, claimed him as its agent only illustrates how UFOs and out-of-the-mind experiences had become interchangeable. Both were 'spaced out'. President Kennedy had called for exploration of the final frontier, outer space. Psychedelia's prophets saw their mission as the exploration of the vast territories of inner space.

But they found footprints. They were not the first and the wilderness was not empty.

By 1974, when the first UK paperback of *The Flying Saucer Vision* was published, Michell felt the need to add a rather apologetic foreword describing the book as "a genuine artefact of 1967". This was ingenuous since the book must have been written before psychedelia flowered in Britain. Yet *Flying Saucer Vision* contained the basic structure of Michell's ideas. In the 1985 interview, his theory of the origin of human intelligence as one in a series of quantum leaps, had not altered since *The Flying Saucer Vision*. "Universal traditions emphasise that the ancient system of knowledge did not come about in the course of evolution, but first appeared in its highest and most

perfect form as an instant revelation from the gods."
Nevertheless he acknowledges that his ideas can vary.
"My present opinion is that the switch lies somewhere
among the strewn wreckage of the ancient canon of
number." He was also open about how he in turn puts
his own message into a personal yet universal code. "I
use Atlantis as a symbol."

If the flying saucer is seen as a symbol then it has
had previous manifestations. "Dragons and Flying
Saucers are invariably interchangeable." He makes an
even greater claim: "The worship of the sacred serpent is
an expression of the flying saucer cult which is the basis
of all religion." Stories involving dragons should be read
as accounts of meetings between mankind and creatures
in fiery flying discs. What happened at those meetings
and where did they take place? They were 'collection
points' where prime humans assembled preparatory to
being taken by the gods. In turn the gods imparted new
wisdom.

This is the core of Michell's philosophy: the transmission of wisdom. In *The Flying Saucer Vision* he
describes various symbols of how wisdom is transmitted.
It is brought by vehicles: the dragon-disc-saucer. The
dragon-serpent is associated in many legends with intro-
ducing knowledge, eg in Eden it twined spirally around
the tree of knowledge of good and evil. Here Michell
offers one of these flashes which are so characteristic:
"The controlled eating of apples may have been a former
mystic practice, designed like the modern use of the
hallucinative mushroom, to give man an insight into
another world."

For Michell the moment when wisdom is transmit-

*The overwhelming visitation — Carl Wilson*

ted is a transcendental one like the supreme act of creation. It can only occur in a flash as a revelation, "a moment of magical inspiration, the coming of the Holy Ghost". As wisdom is a revelation and comes from outside, Michell has no time for any theory of a slow awakening through 'evolution'. Likewise the flash which illuminates is the starting point for all great endeavours like Art.

<hr />

During the two years between *Flying Saucer Vision* and *View Over Atlantis*, Michell appears to have received many such flashes. It is useful to ask how much the mood of 1967 affected Michell rather than vice versa. In February 1968 he gave a lecture[3] which showed how he was incorporating new material into the framework he had laid down in *Flying Saucer Vision*. Three examples show how his thought was developing: 1) He refers to the work of Professor Thom whose book *Megalithic Sites in Britain* had come out after *Flying Saucer Vision*; 2) He enlarges the significance of Watkins; 3) He does not mention *Feng Shui*.

Thom's work provided Michell with the necessary mathematical proofs to justify his theory of the purpose of the sites. Thom's second book *Megalithic Lunar Observatories* in turn developed this thesis. It was beyond dispute that the sites were arranged in relation to the heavens. Thom's work was full of detailed arithmetic and geometry but the implication was simple: there were lines projecting from the stones to the stars. This gave a revelatory importance to the lines which connected the sites and formed "the geometry of the country".

For someone who has become identified with these lines, leys, it is revealing to see how modest was the space given to them in Michell's first book. A cryptic footnote hinted: "Lung Mei, straight lines linking the places associated with the dragons, have recently been traced in Britain." In *Flying Saucer Vision* he had discussed the idea that there were other forms of power by which UFOs flew: "not by engines, but by some natural forces we have not yet discovered". In fact he contradicted this by showing how widespread were cases of flight by humans such as Druids, saints or witches, without any devices or engines. "The belief that sound can cause levitation is old and universal" and Michell suggested that the stones of the Pyramid and Stonehenge were raised by such methods. If harmonious arrangement was capable of producing notes or tones of this strength, then what if the geometry of the earth was laid out in similar patterns? Could it also be used to lift and power craft such as UFOs? Was there a sort of celestial tramline of inaudible energy along which it was possible to fly to and from the sites?

During this interim a transition took place until in *The View Over Atlantis* the emphasis was reversed: the lines are the key and the UFOs incidental. *Flying Saucer Vision* had been full of urgent calls for the recovery and reactivation of the code. By February 1968 the heralds who warned Man are no longer so important. "I think it is time we stopped trying to convince non-believers [about the existence of UFOs] and began to turn our attention to what it is they are pointing out to us." He was now sure they pointed at "the revelations concealed within the landscape itself".

Before the flashes of discovering Feng Shui and numbers[4] Michell had tried to describe the purpose of the code. "The movement of time was recorded at the stone circles; ripples of time spread across the country and from centre to centre across the world. These ripples set in motion all the natural processes of plants, animals and, at one time, man. Men knew when the season, the very hour, had come at which certain things had to be done in accordance with the rhythm of nature. This state of dreamlike certainty thus achieved, liberated the mind into a higher plane, one where time was seen as relative and where actual travel in time was possible and practised." This ability to fly not just in the visible world or on the celestial routes but through other dimensions was a common attribute of holy persons. The psychedelic prophets had aspired to this potential by experimenting with hallucinogens and disciplines. (Those who consider it far-fetched for people to try to project themselves into the future might remember our age is sending unholy sites energised by nuclear waste many hundreds of years into the future.)

UFOs are still the metaphor for "a revelation on such an unsuspected scale it can no way be made to accord with our present attitudes." Or, as in the Conclusion to *Flying Saucer Vision*, Mankind is at one of those critical moments when it receives a quantum leap of intelligence. Michell suggests one way this could come about. "I believe we have the opportunity to develop another organ of perception." Here it is worth noting that, on both proposals, Michell puts a new slant. What UFOs point to is not new but "so huge and obvious that we have overlooked it". Likewise the extra sense is not new but "dormant".

The View Over Atlantis contains both these ideas in its opening paragraph. It describes how Aubrey became aware of a vast ancient temple. "It was not hidden ... yet Aubrey was the first of his age to notice it." The notion that we live in a colossal ruin would have extra poignancy for Englishmen of Michell's generation who had been groomed to be the Platonic guardians for a world empire that no longer existed. Next Michell repeated his central theme: "The instrument of all human enlightenment is an educated mind illuminated by revelation". In the first part of the book he provides example after example of such epiphanies. *View Over Atlantis* bibliography gives an indication of the extra layer which was now laid over the foundations. In particular Michell had found a purpose for the code in the Chinese system of Feng Shui. As he had linked the dragon paths of China with the ley lines of Watkins, so he suggested similarities between the geomancers of China and European magic, especially alchemy and astrology as they had been practised in their heyday during the Renaissance.

Indeed, Michell's call for a Reformation, or Restoration, of the Earth and the Heavens is reminiscent of those appeals for cosmic transformation which characterised the Renaissance. All of them transcend mere political revolution. How the vision is reflected institutionally is another matter. The call is made. *The View Over Atlantis*, with its vision of celestial essences pulsating through all living matter in the universe, is worthy of Böhme. It is the traditional ecstasy which is eternally recognised by mystics and magicians. A holy land is seen stretched out below by a god in the skies who watches rays of divine love streaming to infinity. By the end of the 17th century such dreams of illumination had turned into the Newtonian enlightenment, with universal education as the horizon.

This "sacred engineering" was the purpose of the code. It was a sort of alchemy on a cosmic scale. *View Over Atlantis* showed how such a possibility, far from being Michell's fancy, had been recognised in other times and places. On the one hand it was known to mystical antiquarians like Stukeley and Blake. On the other hand those who dismissed such visionaries as cranks (like UFO believers) had a harder time ignoring the largest country on Earth. The vast landmass of China has always been legendary for its harmonious blend of natural features with the hugest population on the planet. Feng Shui showed this result was not accidental but due to the use of sacred engineering. For Feng Shui was a carefully recorded system of how to harmonise the universe and everything in it.

Clearly, China's successful example could provide the inspiration lacking in the West's new idea of Ecology. These countries might return to the systems of sacred engineering which had once prevailed in their own lands. This was of great urgency as successive utopian schemes, lacking such inspiration, were revealed as having created bigger and nastier conditions. In Britain the mission to destroy slums would lead to the destruction of many ancient landmarks yet provide openings for greed and vanity to erect some of the most hideous buildings known to man.

Such was the importance he attached to Feng Shui that Michell would stimulate a new edition of a study of the system made by a Victorian missionary, Rev. E.J. Eitel. This centenary edition was illustrated by photographs showing the beneficial results of using the system. In the next decade the Eitel would go into three editions and more reprints, and even be sold back to the Chinese.

In *View Over Atlantis* Michell offered a gloss on Jung's idea of changes. "Old secrets rise to the surface and dissolve into the consciousness of the human race to fertilise the seed of evolutionary growth." First published in 1969 *View Over Atlantis* was to prove to be "the right book at the right time" even more than *Flying Saucer Vision*. *View Over Atlantis* gave the New Agers a framework and a programme of practical action. Now they saw not only with the flying saucer vision but also an Atlantean view. Hippies turned themselves into the new guardians of ancient skills and wisdom by rejecting industrial society and communing at old sites or going for mystical nature rambles along ley lines, keeping an eye open for UFOs. Like Red Indians they touched the earth and felt the stones giving off psychic energies or 'vibes'. Some pop groups privately gave invocatory performances at the chosen time and place. It was all mixed up somehow as cosmic consciousness and it gave many people happy hours – all of them charged-up to Michell's book.

*The View Over Atlantis* was to achieve a cult status and the first edition, privately published under Michell's supervision, soon went out of print. This increased the paradox that Michell's ideas were spreading at a time when his books were hard to find. It was three years before *View Over Atlantis* was republished and by then leys had achieved the status of a Subject. *The Ley Hunter* was revived in the winter of 1969, so giving a sort of apostolic succession from Watkins' group. It would appear regularly as a monthly magazine of modest means yet it offered a unique meeting place. The findings of all sorts of enthusiasts filled the early editions: UFOs, leys, psychics. It published splendidly daring theories which have since provided copy for many SF writers. Under new management *TLH* reached its 100th issue in 1986. Amongst the celebrations there was a call for the need for a fresh spirit. Perhaps this relates to its other boast that the subject now contained "several sub-disciplines" as well as a whole discipline, Earth Mysteries, for which 14 departments were listed.

Also in the aftermath of *The View Over Atlantis*, Michell encouraged the reissue of Watkins' original master work **The Old Straight Track** and contributed to a collection of studies published by the Research Into Lost Knowledge Organisation (RILKO). This anthology's subtitle, 'A Study in Patterns', was an accurate description of Michell's new interpretation of the phenomena Jung had called archetypes. Michell viewed the landscape of Britain from above and deciphered a vast secret order spread across the country. Like Watkins he saw a configuration made up by lines connecting ancient sites, earthworks, stones, wells . . . "arranged to demonstrate certain magic properties of the land and sky".

So much research of all sorts was done after the appearance of *View Over Atlantis* that by 1972, when Garnstone Press issued a second edition under its imprint, Michell was able to update some points. This process of revision continued with different editions. More fresh calculations were issued in a small book Ancient Metrology (1981) which may have decided Michell. Less than 10 years after the first Garnstone edition, the volume of new material was so great (including the findings published in a number of periodicals devoted to Michellean topics) that Michell undertook revision on such a scale that he changed the title to The New View Over Atlantis.

In his new Preface Michell reviewed the changes. Though he admitted many additional details, or shifts of emphasis, it is clear that he felt these only strengthened his original framework. "The purpose behind" still remained "the deepest of ancient mysteries." He re-emphasised the deterioration of that knowledge. Though it is possible to see traces in ritual magic and alchemy the 'science' was "practised on a far grander scale and for a more significant purpose". He reiterates two themes. The core of the code: "The prehistoric alchemists were dealing with the earth itself." It is still Feng Shui: they were using it as the means to create an "alchemical fusion" between cosmic energies and the earth spirit. His other theme is how this ambition was passed down the ages in a code which lay behind all creative endeavour and was glimpsed by people such as Plato.

Michell still sees all of these themes in terms of changing the human psyche: "The whole study has some remarkable side-effects, not merely in altering one's view of the past but in conditioning one's mind in sympathy with that of the ancients." Here he is back in the area

Jung investigated. Michell's 1983 Preface elevates leys to the level of UFOs. Both are "portents of a great seasonal change in mental attitude". By seasonal both Jung and Michell refer to the astrological calendar in which "an event traditionally occurs every 2160 years".

As with *Flying Saucer Vision* so with *View Over Atlantis* — a late addition as the book went to press indicated the next direction. A postscript, 'The Holy Spirit', was provoked by the publication of a book on dowsing. The well-known ability of certain people to divine water suggested an idea on various levels. In the highest sense divining is like anamorphic art and Michell would use his intelligence as a magic mirror to divine the shapes behind the shapes.

*The View Over Atlantis* spoke of "vast crystalline shapes" visible in the landscape. In his third book, City of Revelation, Michell provided a synthesis of his first two books by crystallising his ideas. It was as if pillars of light drove up from the framework he had laid out to form the ultimate symbol: the holy city. Ideas came off the page like psychedelic devices to shimmer through the consciousness of his readers. I deliberately use extravagant language in an effort to recreate the impact Michell's early works had on their admirers. They not only caused the flash which illuminates hidden vistas but retransmitted the experience so that they triggered flashes in the minds of his readers. For many the discovery of Michell's ideas was to be an indelible experience. It was a device which opened their minds to wonder.

Despite this emotional response to his work Michell

was becoming more exacting and precise. *City of Revelation* abounds in shapes, measures, numbers, proportions and harmonies. From the figures spread across the landscape he turned to the figures which unlock all codes: numbers. In a way Numerology plays the same role as UFOs and leys but it goes further as it is the key to unravel all the secrets, of Earth and Heaven. The interchangeability, or use of metaphor, had found an exact system.

Michell uses the cabbalists' code of Gematria which breaks down language to individual letters and assigns them numerical equivalents. In fact this is one part of an incredibly complex system, or systems, which have been used for centuries. As early as 1300 the mystic Ramon Lull had devised a series of wheels as a kind of early computer to integrate his variations as he attempted to reconcile Christian, Jewish, Moslem and Gnostic values. Michell's attempt to square the circle mixed the Holy City of Jewish-Christian apocalyptic tradition with the Ideal State of Plato's *Republic*.

The idea of correspondence has other ramifications. The doctrine of signatures was obligatory for astrologers, magicians and doctors, while poetic myth, as explored by Robert Graves, adds more parallels in flowers, trees, herbs, colours, sounds, gems ... This infinity of permutations applied to everything in the universe from its innermost structure, like DNA code, or to the outer stars. The idea mentioned in *Flying Saucer Vision* of harmonics linked to a power which enabled flight was now put into a larger structure. All the ancient holy sites, not only Stonehenge and the Pyramids, evidenced this code. Their successors, the cathedrals, had inherited not only the sites but also were instruments which expressed this magical canon.

As though in a flash it appeared this code, or canon, was not only everywhere but it had only recently been ignored. It transpired the code, as passed down the ages, was a well-known tradition: it was canonical. By the early 1970s academic attitudes to Renaissance magic had been transformed by Frances Yates and others. For example, they showed how a magico-mystical system, as Vitruvianism, has inspired both the architectural glories of ancient Rome and of the Palladians. Could the neglect of this code, or its deliberate flouting to the extent of using a basic unit of measure hostile to Man, have any bearing on why people were instinctively repelled by modern buildings?

*The View Over Atlantis* found its system in Feng Shui; *City of Revelation* had its canon. Each offered a code which could manipulate the universe. Perhaps Michell's spell in Intelligence had born ironic fruit.

On the surface *City of Revelation* was harder to assimilate. Anybody could draw lines on a map, but calculating numbers demanded mental effort. The other immediate impression was conveyed by the diagrams: number expressed geometrically produced powerful images. Even those ignorant of the origin of these patterns might, as with ley lines, think they were not seeing something new but being reminded of something with which they had always been familiar on an instinctive level. Jung's archetypes again provide a starting point as the diagrams have an harmonious effect reminiscent of mandalas. Jung likened flying saucers to mandalas or circles of power. In the diagramatic codes of *City of Revelation* Michell offered another linking point through which many currents might flow. Another image evoked by the patterns in *City of Revelation* was the seals or pentacles used in magic. This is not far-fetched as Michell's use of Number also relies on magic squares as well as on the cabbalistic system.

Two new permutations arise: (1) That the lines described in *View Over Atlantis* are not random but form recognisable patterns. By the same token the symbols of magic are codified versions of the patterns laid on the Earth. (2) That there is an even deeper pattern which takes us into the structure of language via number. Here Michell is working in that part of the Platonic tradition followed by Gnostics, Alchemists and neo-Platonists like Thomas Taylor.

In an essay published in 1969 Michell had argued that "Agreement is illusion, harmony is reality."[5] By using Number in this mystical way he could demonstrate these truths. As he had used UFOs, leys, and Atlantis as symbols, so the ultimate ambition of squaring the circle could stand for the reconciling of the irreconcilable. It was all done by Numbers. Contradictory or opposing phenomena could have the same number: eg 666 was the number of the Beast *and* Christ.

As one person could appear as a genius to his supporters, to his opponents he was mad. By the early 1970s the psychedelic movement exhibited this Janus quality. The idea of separating from the evil society of Amerika (*sic*) had produced over 2,000 drop-out communities.[6] At the gathering of these white tribes for a concert at Woodstock an activist called for the declaration of the existence of a separate Nation. Simultaneously one of this nation's tribes, the Mansonites, was hacking to death celebrities in Hollywood.

Another reversal of a different shape was discernable. Archaeological orthodoxy was switching under various attacks, including that of the Michelleans. By 1974 his books were easily available and few 'mystical scenes' magazines did not show the influence of Michell's thought. Universities had begun to regard themselves as citadels of dogma rather than of imagination, and they found the new students coming with heretical ideas in their minds. The first Department to react was Archaeology. Tests cases were fought in journals and public debate. One battle was over the suggestion that the sites have a much older history. Because they had been adapted by Christianity there had been a literal cover-up. Following this exposure came the next logical battle. As the sites showed evidence of superior mathematical ability then, *QED*, primitive man was not ape-like but intelligent. He was our superior.

This fitted with Michell's original proposition as the people of the Past were now revealed to be as alien as the aliens from elsewhere who had transmitted the spark of intelligence. Another piece of the pattern was also confirmed: that the wisdom has always been here, waiting to be unearthed when the time is ripe.

Once the wisdom is received how should it be re-transmitted? As it is already in a pattern or code it can be left for every age to rediscover. Here we are near Jung's idea of archetypes, but with a very different purpose.

48.

**Drawn for the Sunday Times April 5th 1964.**

**Drawn for the National Geographic Magazine.**

**Drawn for a scientific journal.**

**Our choice**

*Different views of the same evidence: man or monster?*
*— The Fanatic*

Here the secret, or canon, provides the key. It is the codification of the previous visitation — when Man became intelligent. Now Man is about to make a new leap of equally amazing proportions and this code is the sole apparatus for receiving the new transfiguration.

For Michell the moment of receiving intelligence is apocalyptic. It is so transcendent, overwhelming and indelible that it negates all civilization both Present and Past. All restraints are obsolete and all laws must be denied. This is a wild imperative. That way lies anarchy and madness. Yet Michell's other exhortation is that civilization is based on an age-old code.

The Janus head offers contradictory faces or the simultaneous presence of opposites. On the one hand everything Man has achieved since he became intelligent is to be swept away in a flash. On the other hand all humanity's greatest achievements express this inner secret.

Actually there is a proviso. Like many others Michell questions modern civilization. For him it is not a matter of building an internal critique — the basis is wrong. The overwhelming evidence points to the present civilization of the West as being an exception to the universal rule. It is the freak while the 'freaks' are the norm. Applying this thought pattern to other arguments produces startling new perspectives on problems which seem intractable. Tribal Man still practices the traditional beliefs. He is at one with the universe, not its master. He regards the Earth as an organism not a machine. It was these primitive superstitions which had justified the extermination of the people who held them. Seen in this way Darwinism is more than racism. The scientific and philosophical framework, synthesised as Darwinism, is one side in a war between contradictory cosmologies. Anybody suspected of fellow-travelling with Tribal cosmology — whether Red Indians, British folklore, or hippies at Stonehenge — is guilty of endangering the basis of modern civilization.

As usual with mystics Michell is accused of being head-in-air and impractical. Yet, also as usual with mystics, the power of their vision calls for a more fundamental transformation than any revolutionary.

In fact Michell was to set out on a range of campaigns which were highly topical and political in the profoundest sense. Characteristically he chose a distinctive and traditional vehicle: the art of pamphleteering as it had been in its heyday at the time of Swift.

*City of Revelation* had shown how everything has its numerical value. *View Over Atlantis* had dealt in the importance of proportion for producing harmonious relationships. All the patterns depended on dimensions, which meant measurement held the universe together. As the cosmos is one so everything is inter-related and has its proportionate place. Otherwise all the shapes would become distorted, buildings would be inhuman, people would grow monstrous, the land would turn grotesque, and life be betrayed. If measurement was the difference between cosmic harmony or universal anarchy what was to be the basic unit of measure?

In Spring 1972 Michell issued his first 'Radical Traditionalist Paper' which provided **A Defence of Sacred Measures**. The concept of the series encapsulated his outlook. As always he saw himself as the proponent of eternal orthodoxy against a recent exception made for reasons professedly antagonistic to Mankind. The pamphlet was hawked in the old way and it drew him into a campaign of his own. Two other Radical Traditionalist Papers followed in the next months on tangential topics, but the main concern was the fight against the imposition of an alien and atheistic system. In the following years he wrote to the newspapers, elevated himself as Chairman of the Anti-Metrication Board, produced five issues of its newsletter, **The Just Measure**, reprinted another author's pamphlet which argued the same case, and inspired a grand garden fete and rally at which traditional measures were celebrated in true Peacock style. The campaign was a classic of English character, exhibiting all the high spirits and good humour on which our way of life rests.

This taste for high campaigning was boosted by the battle with Archaeological orthodoxy. Challenged that his ideas were fancies because leys were projections of an over-active imagination (like Jung's UFOs), Michell produced a meticulously documented case study of The Old Stones of Land's End. Yet the opposition was itself in disarray as he noted in the Preface to a new edition of a Victorian study of another megalithic complex, Maeshowe. "For many years until quite recently the theory that the ancient inhabitants of Britain practised the science of astronomy and erected megalithic structures for that purpose was bitterly disputed by almost every respectable archaeologist. Modern research has, however, established beyond doubt that such was indeed the case, and the further surprising evidence has emerged from the new, refined techniques of dating ancient artefacts, that the stone monuments of Britain, Scandinavia and Brittany are older than those of southern Europe, the Mediterranean and Egypt. The long held orthodox belief that civilization spread from Egypt or Mesopotamia to northern Europe is thus reversed."

The note of glee was continued in a witty squib written at this time, A Little History of Astro-Archaeology. This showed how orthodoxy switched to heresy and vice versa. *City of Revelation* had used Number to show how a phenomenon can be viewed simultaneously as good and evil. *The Souvenir Programme*, also from this time, contained the idea of a Janus head which simultaneously exhibits contradictory faces. *Little History of Astro-Archaeology* developed these paradoxes further to show how a line could go in a circle: orthodoxy became heresy and vice versa. But a line could form a loop, a reverse loop or a spiral. Michell was treating beliefs as phenomena: ideas had patterns, thoughts had shapes and fashions in opinion were measurable. He turned the Jungian idea of 'treating' a belief system against the idea of orthodoxy itself: orthodoxy was only one more belief system. Reality was a condition. With hilarious results he showed how irrational was the belief in rationality. A system of orthodox reality which had been rock-hard in its rejection of any different ideas could not only crumble but accept and preach previous heresies with equal dogmatism.

To illustrate the ephemeral nature of orthodoxy, Michell chose the official line of the SS on mystical sites! This had many implications, all of them mischievous. Rarely has an orthodoxy been imposed

with more cruelty — and it was magico-mysticism!
*Little History of Astro-Archaeology* faced the accusation
that such beliefs and meddling in occultism could lead to
'dangerous politics'. It showed the SS in a different light,
as the patron of mystics. In turn this reminded contem-
porary worshippers of such beliefs that the policy had
seemed the height of enlightenment. Others had
regarded it as the epitome of evil. Mystics and occultists
who yearned to be in power could see a precedent. By
using this paradoxical combination Michell warned those
who believed themselves to be gentle sensitive souls
above suspicion that Himmler could be portrayed as one
of their number. Smug dismissals of Hitler as a person
demonically inspired could backfire.

As orthodoxy and heresy could be interchangeable,
so a person or thing could be perceived in opposite ways.
In 1973 a figure from the era of liberated London was
under sentence of death. The case of Michael X — the
English version of Malcolm X — attracted luminaries
from the new aristocracy of opinionators such as the
feminist Kate Millet, pop idol John Lennon and his wife
Oh No!, the artist of embarrassment. As friends of
Michael's from the idealistic days of the 1960s, John
Michell and Bill Levy, an early editor of *IT*, produced a
booklet which put the case in a different way. The cover
continued the style of explanatory titles begun by the
Rad Trad papers: **Souvenir Programme for the Official
Lynching of Michael Abdul Malik** *with poems, stories,
sayings by the Condemned. Fully illustrated.* In fact it
was so different it caused its own stir and was a sign of
the changes which had overtaken 'the alternative society'.
Its publishers, who had previously been eager to produce

a book by Michell, refused to be associated with the project. It seemed Michell's work was acceptable if it was non-political. This was a twist on the previous criticism that it was not political enough. *The Souvenir Programme* was accused of 'racism and sexism'. A new orthodoxy was imposing itself. There was a double irony since the subject of the campaign was ambivalent and hardly an acceptable hero — except to the new orthodox.

For by 1973 'all you need is love' had become 'armed love'. Posters of hippies with guns promoted the message of enforcing love as freedom fighters. Newspeak ruled. 'Expanded consciousness' had become the sales pitch of dope merchants while 'cosmic' marketed everything from jewellery and perfume to cars and music. New prophets competed with each other, all fiercely intolerant of anybody who didn't love properly or who fell short of their ideals. The murders by the Manson tribe found apologists, as did the murders attributed to Michael's group. This Newspeak, love=hate, embraced not just the established order but those who showed insufficient ideological soundness. Rhetoric had supplied a new pattern: the abstract Cause or instant '-ism'. All bigots had unlimited opportunities for expressing their hostility and cruelty in the name of liberation. This changed mood was encapsulated by Michell and Levy in a poster promoting their booklet under the slogan Will Causism hang Michael X?. Michael's appeal was rejected and the execution hastily carried out. That he has not been turned into a martyr but was rapidly forgotten is indicative of the new impotence and hypocrisy.

*The Souvenir Programme* had not presented Michael in a causist costume but had described him in terms of character. He was offered as an example of a person who, after seeing the light (UFOs, drugs, leys, a new world, whatever), can no longer return to their former ways. An indelible experience means they can only see in the new way, with a different perception like Flying Saucer vision. Afterwards they are 'driven' just as much as Dostoyevsky's characters are possessed. Having explored this phenomenon in Michael, Michell would offer more 'cases': J.T. Blight, Artaud, Strindberg, Hitler. This list could be grouped as notoriously wicked persons or notoriously mad men. *Flying Saucer Vision* had dealt with a notoriously mad idea. Indeed *View Over Atlantis* had contained gentler examples, including Alfred Watkins, the respectable businessman who ended his life notoriously devoted to his crank theory.

[AN INTERLUDE as the author offers some excuses]

A frequent problem for mystics, unlike driven people, is the impossibility of keeping excitement at a peak. I suggest Michell's work did not suffer this fate because the expectations were lowered by others. Commercialisation literalised the psychedelic dream. The Age of Aquarius became a song and dance number as the anthem of *Hair*. The New Age was not remarkably different: there was no increase or decrease in conflict. The commercial world turned psychedelia into a rhetoric of fashion: hairstyles, clothes, music, graphics. All were images, outward forms, which could not change the human psyche. Like any husk they were powerless without inspiration.

Michell's work had a measurable impact on the subjects it touched. After *Flying Saucer Vision* the Adamski genre had become a period piece. Saucerites either adapted or faced oblivion. Eventually a variant was found which revamped the mixture as *Is God An Astronaut?* Once more the subject could be sensationalised. Astronaut cultists were found in other countries. In Britain, Von Daniken's theories were serialised by a Sunday paper notorious for its revelations about human irregularities. God was finally exposed as a little old green man.

Another form of literalism defused expectations. The causists had become fanatical about forms. All that counted was the catechism of orthodoxy. Wisdom, having been achieved, was finite. There was no need for a further transformation which would break the mould and allow the currents to flow and inspire a new revelation. It was the same old story. These causists believed in themselves so blindly they became more self-righteous, pompous and humourless than their opponents. Previously heretical opinion and behaviour was now proclaimed as normal and orthodox. With no hint of irony, the causists promoted perversion, sin and crime. Hardline politics recognised only hardline occultism. Ironically all this dogmatism proved Michell's point that freedom's other face is tyranny. If opposing ideas about human destiny could be interchangeable then political fanaticism was even funnier.

As commerce seized on the exploitable element of the vision and causism on its comforting certainty, so another sort of literalism further lowered the high-minded imagery. Michell's concern for wisdom as intelligence or truth had made him publicise his findings in every possible way. Though truth is open and universal, to those with closed minds it appears secret and selective. This mentality, seeing truth as a mystery, projects the existence of "hidden streams of esoteric truth" handed down by an "arcane tradition". *City of Revelation* had referred to those who worship the Image of the Beast. It is a vital distinction as it shows it is the image which is evil, hence the first commandment. In the same way, the tree of the knowledge of good and evil is quite different from a Tree of Good and Evil.

This theory that the secrets of the universe must be a mystery only for initiates encouraged two ideas. First: the traditional paranoia about secret societies. This revitalised interest in the Masons and other old favourites like the Rosicrucians or Jesuits. Second: the negative side of this notion provoked a craze for conspiracy theories. By the mid-1970s a generation had grown accustomed to the proposition that any official version was a lie. Just as regimes had to be overthrown by freedom fighters, so the system of lies had to be overthrown by the bearer of truth. The Watergate scandal brought such paranoiacs to a frenzy.

Michell's work seems peculiarly vulnerable to 'interpretation'. As he uncovers 'secrets', so he is reputed to be peddling secrets. With each title he produced a group appeared which preached the image. At the time of *Flying Saucer Vision* a society called for the training of watchers on mountain peaks who would receive messages from superior alien visitors. Its rhetoric warned that if its call was neglected Mankind would perish. *View Over Atlantis* was followed by ley cultists. *City of Revelation* was answered by a craze for numbers. *Feng Shui* evoked institutes of geomancers and engineers with gadgets. *Old*

*Stones of Land's End* found stone finders. Comments on Glastonbury discovered zodiacs and other figures. *Earth Spirit* turned up concern for all sorts of forces. Even his pamphleteering awakened unsuspected enthusiasm for measures and creationism. *Phenomena* and its sequel, though co-authored with the editor of *Fortean Times*, spawned a monthly of *Curious Facts*. If all these images are taken at surface value Michell's work appears as a parade of crankiness. Because he writes about leys or ufos he should not be assumed to be their adherent any more than writing about Hitler makes him a Nazi. Michell's own words prove he has a deeper purpose. He is dealing with the sublime while the literalists rejoice in the ridiculous.

This imitation had two causes. Some thought Michell's work was too clever and should be popularised and made commercially rewarding. Similar arguments had reduced psychedelia to ingredients which could be mass-produced cheaply. *The Thing* could produce images of anything. During the 1970s everything had to be revised to the latest sensibility. Just as a revolution re-writes history so culture had to be dressed in the new costumes. Christianity needed to be rock-and-roll-ised. Or disco-fied. Michell's ideas would be disco-fied by the commercial faithful.

Other popularisers were plagiarising for the highest motives. Michell himself has commented on how many people "recognise" the ideas he puts forward as their own. These people feel these ideas deeply and instinctively though previously they were 'held' unconsciously. After these ideas have been made visible people feel the need to confirm their ancient beliefs, often by writing them out again as a devotee repeats scripture. Were these people projecting after a sighting? Their adherence to unfashionable opinions suggests they are experiencing a Michellean vision.

*Flying Saucer Vision* had discussed the idea of döppelgangers as used by writers like Dostoyevsky. (Note the context was literary not the part-science, part-philosophy which became the trademark of Colin Wilson.) In *Souvenir Programme* and *A Little History of Astro-Archaeology* Michell had refined his ideas. One person could be a double. In the same way contradictory interpretations could be projected onto one idea. This phenomenon is not peculiar to Michell. Other mystical quests reflect this response. Some saw Alchemy as a way to spiritual transfiguration while others attempted to turn dross into gold. Those who sought earthly riches were known as Puffers. Cabbalists showed they had attained a certain proficiency or level of initiatory wisdom by ceremonially creating a golem which they then destroyed. The idea of making a mechanical slave was in complete contrast to the ability to share in the act of Creation. Magicians who transformed reality had their pale reflections in conjurors who relied on sleight of hand to trick the gullible.

As the *Souvenir Programme* had been seen in opposite ways so Michell would be regarded in opposite ways. For his detractors the *Souvenir Programme* closed the case: his politics were reactionary and evil. As with the old so with the new. Michell continued to proclaim himself as the prophet of eternal orthodoxy whilst his detractors were heretics, cranks and fanatics.

---

*Sharing a love of Cornwall*

Michell was still regarded as the great heretic and could no longer rely on finding favour with the many new 'underground' magazines. More and more he turned to other independent spirits and ventures and gave them his encouragement. Apart from the RILKO Organisation his occasional pieces were published by newly formed small outfits like Zodiac House and The Land of Cokaygne. The Elephant Press of Cornwall produced the most lavish edition of any of Michell's books: de-luxe handmade copies of the *Old Stones of Land's End.* These were made available by another old-fashioned system: subscription only.

Michell's affection for this part of the country which retains much of its old culture, customs, language, outlook and — most visibly — its stones, would be apparent in another book of local interest. A Short Life at the Land's End was exquisitely produced, again by private methods. The essay on the life and work of the greatest illustrator of Cornish stones and scenes marked another development in Michell's work. The subject, J.T. Blight, was a kind of romantic failure rather in the Chatterton mould as, after his early explosion of illustrating, he became a noted lunatic. Michell developed his notion that those who are touched by the spirit, like UFOs or any other form of transcendence, can only follow their vision which may lead them to their doom. A poignant addition revealed Blight did not die romantically, young wild and dashing, but was kept quietly in an asylum until his natural death in old age. Yet as a case study *A Short Life at the Land's End* offered an example of how peculiar notions affected an eccentric life. Blight was a sort of freak, an outcrop, on the Cornish historical landscape.

In the years following *City of Revelation* Michell
had campaigned vigorously for his views, not least by
offering case studies or proofs such as *Old Stones of
Land's End* and *Maeshowe*. He had always acknowledged
and promoted his inspirational sources, often encouraging
their works being put back into print — e.g. Eitel,
Watkins, Stirling. His influence was apparent on Garnstone Press which began to republish other canonical
works on old stone crosses, old roads, and a memoir of
Watkins by his elderly son Allen. Under his own imprint,
West Country Editions, Michell reissued a study on
**Bladud** the Druid ruler of Bath, who was famous for his
ability to fly. In a way this was another case-study by an
earlier author so it could not be attributed to Michell's
imagination. Published for the celebrations of Bath as a
Roman centre, this reminder of the city's more ancient
and beneficial history also helped to save the hot springs
long renowned for their curative properties. That the
transformative qualities in the pattern on the landscape
might relate to similar powers in the earth itself had
been mooted in *View Over Atlantis*. The idea of a form
of sacred engineering had been developed in the crucial
concluding essay of *Old Stones of Land's End*. It was
now refined in **The Earth Spirit**.

By 1971 a new market had been reported by the
*Observer*. Its article appeared in October 1972 as 'The
Spirit World is now available over the counter'. Even this
'boom' was overtaken in 1975 by which time the
pioneer booksellers and publishers had been made
redundant by a transformation of the book trade. By the
mid-1970s the 'underground' was available over the
counter. 'Counter-culture' was big business and its
originators could put up or shut up.

Amongst the major publishing houses which joined this trend was Thames and Hudson. It had the reputation of being one of the foremost art book publishers and was thus ideally placed to produce quality pictorial paperbacks at a popular price. Thames and Hudson had launched a new series, 'Art and Imagination', which offered illustrated essays on specific aspects of the new mysticism. These took the form of a short introductory essay and a mass of pictures, some in colour, many with captions. The packaging was perfect.

One in this series was *The Earth Spirit*. Michell was faced with the prospect of exploiting the market his own work had created. By now each of his titles spawned its cultists: UFO freaks, leyline hunters, stones students, number collectors — and now an entirely new subject: Earth Mysteries. The battle between the apostles of Earth Mysteries and academic orthodoxy raged mainly over Archaeology and Astronomy. As predicted in *A Little History of Astro-Archaeology*, the dogmatists of both sides began to cross over. The academics allowed a scientific purpose to the temples of the stars while the psychic engineers measured their claims and success in terms of gadgets.

The idea that the Earth itself could be revitalised by a spirit as a sort of current was the basis of *Feng Shui*. In turn this switch might also transform society and Mankind. On the individual level such a total change was the phenomenon already explored as the indelible experience which makes people 'driven'. The psychedelic prophets had wondered if this change in vision, in intelligence, could be so permeating that it was biological. If so, could similar patterns be found in Nature? What about the freaks for which orthodox science has no explanation?

A peak of Michell's unorthodox publishing was reached in 1975. At the same time that his campaign for traditional measures and English values climaxed in the Anti-Metric Fete so his other use of tradition, the pamphlet style and form, came to a high point. Turning the accusations back against their originators, Michell produced a unique magazine rejoicing in the wonderfully ironic name of The Fanatic. Everything was reversed. Labelled a heretic, Michell took the idea at face value and explored the state of play.

His co-author of the offensive *Souvenir Programme*, Bill Levy, would also produce a lethal *Fanatic*. A bumper *Fanatic* would be issued under the aegis of other friends, Heathcote Williams and Richard Adams of Open Head Press. This team had commissioned two rubber stamps for printing the slogans CRANK MAIL and UNSOLICITED. Stamped on all mail they sent out these legends gave the appearance of official approval. Not only did this encourage paranoia in recipients about the all-seeing eye of the authorities, but it voiced the sentiments secretly held about their work.

*The Fanatic*'s front cover read like a huge pamphlet title or a manifesto of contents. "Things don't look quite so steady as they did — the FANATIC will come out with increasing frequency until the promise is kept." Apart from describing the Appearance of the New Jerusalem on Earth, the magazine also reprinted the text of *Rad Trad* No. 2 which ended with a long extract from the Book of Revelations: "Babylon the great is fallen, and is become the habitation of devils, and the hold of every foul spirit, and a cage of every unclean and hateful bird. . . "

The same sort of mind-spinning impact was made by the cover of Phenomena, *a book of wonders*. This was published in 1977 by which time Hollywood had caught up with Michell's first metaphor. The film *Close Encounters of the Third Kind* was a textbook case of a person who has an indelible experience (his face is burnt) and who becomes 'driven'. This obsession leads him to penetrate the official international conspiracy and to find that aliens are communicating with Man on a mountain top (the Devil's Table). The little green creatures (angels? devils?) take away human specimens, including the hero who regards this with supreme bliss.

Reference has been made to the regurgitation of Michell's vision by admirers and plagiarists. The market had demanded that Michell should perform his own image as a party piece. Now Hollywood? Just in time he found a new metaphor. All the leads in the many ventures and publications described above now came together. The *Souvenir Programme* had shown how a person could be regarded as good or evil. *Little History of Astro-Archaeology* had explored the idea that opposing beliefs can find conclusive proofs of the rightness of their cause. *The Fanatic* had synthesised these impulses. "Explanationism is a disease of cranks which makes them explain everything in terms of their pet theory." If proofs could always be found to support any idea then were people reading what they wanted to into the 'evidence'? Or projecting as Jung believed? In *Phenomena* Michell returned to an author he had mentioned in *Flying Saucer Vision*, the American

Charles Fort, who is often dismissed as a humourist. Fort spent years recording proofs (of the inadequacy of orthodox explanations) until he reached the conclusion that proof itself is ridiculous. Having achieved this enlightened state he destroyed his own collection of proofs. This proposition took Michell to another Platonic idea: that the universe obligingly reflects back any image. As people project their desires so the universe reflects back confirmations.

The form of the book was a blend of Thames and Hudson illustrated essay and an old-fashioned crank's compendium. Michell and his co-author Bob Rickard, the editor of *Fortean Times*, offered a five-and-a-half page introductory essay 'The Phenomenal World' and then set out an amazing display of impossibilities. Those who lived in a world which they were confident UFOs could never enter, in which they were not surrounded by landscape geometry, suddenly found they were infested by all sorts of weirdness. Worse, this weirdness had always gone on and would continue. It was happening now. Far worse, this weirdness was exactly the sort of psychic disturbance that meant ordinary people (like you, dear reader) spontaneously combusted (a very indelible experience), spontaneously zoomed into the air, and that even animals could not be relied on to behave properly. Attacks on orthodoxy were shamed by this catalogue of unconventionality. At the same time the presentation and easily digestible captions attracted a mass audience. The sort of sensation seekers who in America buy lurid items like the *National Enquirer* (SHOCK HORROR – BOY HEARS WITH HIS EARS!) or goggle at freak shows, could get their money's worth.

Yet the book had as serious a purpose as *The View Over Atlantis* and would prove to be as important in the development of Michell's ideas.

Far from being an exception *Phenomena* was to provoke a range of new possibilities not least for Michell himself. Where next? An article 'Curious Marks' in *IT* (1978) gave an answer. What about another sort of manifestation; those odd shapes and patterns which are dismissed as 'freaks of Nature'? Were they accidents? Coincidences? Projections? Were they produced spontaneously? *Phenomena* had dealt with cases such as animals, usually toads or frogs, being found inside rock. Here was a puzzle which would have delighted those ancients who read Ovid's *Metamorphoses*. The *Fanatic* had challenged Darwinism with the idea of likenesses in Nature. *The View Over Atlantis* and *City of Revelation* had discussed the geometrical shapes and patterns visible in the landscape. In Nature these patterns or shapes are called simulacra.

*Simulacra* investigated similar formations in matter itself. If leys were visible to Watkins who became a gently driven man, what sort of person noticed these wild oddities? Michell offered two men famed as mad geniuses: Artaud and Strindberg. Both were bywords for being 'driven' and Strindberg's obsession was practising alchemy.

Could the idea that the Earth is covered in a system of marks go further? What if the marks are not artificial but natural? This had enormous implications. *Simulacra* approached the question by examining archetypes in Nature, ie the undeniable recurrent patterns, and asked if they could be generated spontaneously. Simulacra could serve as a sort of geological and botanical metaphor. They offered another way of considering Jung's theory of mental or psychic projections. Are simulacra, like UFOs, the result of psychic disturbances?

The third enquiry into natural oddities was even more fancifully and humorously presented. Posing as a kind of graphic fantasy book of the sort then successful, Inventorum Natura was published by a firm noted for this type of product. The body of the book consisted of full colour illustrations of exotic flora and fauna. They were the sort regularly invented in Science Fiction and Fantasy and the illustrator, Una Woodruff, was known for her work in this genre. The accompanying text was even more like glorifed captions. The introduction by Michell told of what purported to be a newly-discovered work by the Latin author Pliny who had described unconventional species.

Such had been the popular success of *Phenomena* that its publishers commissioned Phenomena 2. Living Wonders was effectively Michell's fourth excursion into this Fortean arena, again with Bob Rickard. It repeated the earlier formula and was even more reticent about drawing any conclusions. The introduction, 'A Little History of Cryptobiology' ended: "In the annals of natural history are many types of reports and anecdotes which, for all their apparent irrationalities, occur again and again in different cultures and periods of time. In some of these is an evident archetypal quality, leading us to suspect that the data on which our understanding of nature is based is as much a product of human nature and the human mind as it is of the world around us."

Though Michell had delivered 'hits' to his new loyal publishers, Thames and Hudson, nevertheless some of his books seemed too off-beat. Indeed his views were as awkward as ever and his taste for voicing them independently persisted. His campaign against metrication as a new expedient system of benefit only to vested interests found its echo in the instinctive common sense of the British who simply ignored the new measures. The possibility of coercion, always threatened by metrication's advocates, seemed repugnant to the new Conservatives who opposed state interference and elevated old values. A similar threat to metricate America was rebuffed in the spirit of sturdy independence. Michell's campaign was to be the inspiration of a similar campaign in the USA from 1979 which resulted in a transatlantic alliance of scorn for any such nonsense.[8] A decade after the Garden Fete, metrication is still regarded as a supreme crankery, and it can only be found where stealth has prevailed. By contrast Architecture has publically repented and its orthodoxy now uses the rhetoric of its opponents of the 1960s. In June 1986 the *Observer* reported that tower blocks which have nothing wrong with them structurally are to be demolished for 'aesthetic reasons'. One Conservative council's aim it to make its area a 'tower-free zone' by destroying seven more blocks.

During his visits to give talks in America, Michell was welcomed as his ideas had provoked a new interest in that country's sacred sites and antiquities. The small circulation magazine which accompanied his talks in the New World bore the name *Un Autre Monde* which had previously been the subtitle of *The Fanatic*. Unfortunately his neologism 'astro-archaeology' was inverted by the Americans. The understandable confusion between astro-archaeology and archaeo-astronomy led to both terms dropping out of usage. Even less understood was another of Michell's private publications. **The Hip Pocket Hitler** was a hip-pocket sized booklet offered in New York in the summer of 1976. This was a militant moment as Jews paraded outside the UN shouting slogans like "Every Jew buy a point two-two". Michell's compilation of quotes from Hitler appeared calculated to cause maximum offence. In fact it did precisely what its blurb claimed: "Of all personages with high media exposure, from Mao to Billy Carter, he [Hitler] alone has been denied the publication of a little book of opinions and epigrams". Of course this could be thought of as gauche, since Hitler's "opinions and epigrams" bombarded the world for many years. Given there is mischief in the pairing of Mao with Billy Carter, it seems, from the context of this essay, that there was a serious intention to this book. Gauche is hardly the adjective to describe a character who is as crafty as Michell. As with *A Little History of Astro-Archaeology's* description of the SS attitude to occultists, some contemporaries might find their views identical with Hitler's eg vegetarianism. Really there are two deeper themes: that of the 'driven' person, and that of the way people project their own values — in this case good or evil. This is not to suggest Michell claims good and evil are the same but that anything, or person, can be perceived in contradictory ways. It all depends on which way you look, positively or negatively. In simple terms it is possible to find good and bad in all of us. In fact Michell is turning ideas on their heads. This is part of his mystical impulse to turn everything upside-down — a wildness which dwarfs revolutionaries like Hitler.

Though his supporters have tried to dismiss such outbursts as mischievous excrescences or 'non canonical'(!), they have earned Michell an unenviable reputation. It is interesting to note Michell's opinion of how unacceptable views should treat censorship. For him it does not exist because he considers a true writer can get any message across without the authorities realising. This reminds us how his work deals in the idea of codes. It should therefore warn us that he may be using a subversive Aesopian language of symbols and metaphors. Another trick is to take advantage of the Janus head quality. A writer can describe something in terms which evoke hostile or sympathetic reactions. Clearly this applies to Hitler, but we can see a breath-taking example in the *Souvenir Programme*. Speaking of his friend's creative talents he writes: "Michael's glib tongue encouraged tenants to give vacant possession." This refers to Michael's notoriety as the evicting agent for an infamous slum landlord. Turning the other cheek of the Janus head would show Michael to have been more associated with thugs, dogs and brutality than a 'charmed tongue'. How did the new orthodoxy cope with that one?

Returning to Michell's case there is an irony in the proposition that such views demean the respectable author of books about flying saucers and ley-lines.

If Michell had been involved in controversy over his booklets on Michael X and Hitler, his contribution to another campaign in 1977 won him more praise and fury. The champion of English Decency, Mrs Whitehouse, had provoked a court case against the leading UK weekly for homosexuals, *Gay News*. Her pretext for this harassment was her objection to a poem which referred to the cock of Christ. At a time when the monarch had publicly joined in the distaste at a film which proposed to show Our Lord's sex life, this issue carried weight. As the laws against buggery had only been repealed in 1968 there were understandable fears. As with the Michael case, Michell's support was to prove an embarrassment. Rather than follow the new orthodoxy's line that no offence was intended, he proclaimed on his pamphlet's cover: **To Represent Our Saviour as "that great cock"** (Kirkup — *Gay News*) is not **Blasphemy** *but Eternal and Christian Orthodoxy*. The pamphlet boasted "irrefutable illustrative proofs" which could be construed as gross indecencies and blasphemies in their own right. Once more Michell was completely at odds with the official version and the alternative orthodoxy.

Michell had already gone wrong in 'sexual politics' with the Michael book. The Cock pamphlet only confirmed his craziness. Yet it was an error he had long held and with reason. Radical Traditionalist Papers No.2 **A Defence of People and Population** had been issued as an antidote to what Michell called Anti-Population Day. This was his name for the celebrations held in May 1973 for Malthus in Bath. Then a resident of that city, Michell and his friends had held their own celebration in protest against the elevation of ideas which had ushered in the worst excesses of the Industrial Revolution. In the guise of Ecology, Malthusianism was making a comeback as alarmists prophesied the Earth's resources of food,

energy and space were on the verge of exhaustion due to over-population. Their solution was truly Malthusian: sterilisation. Such a programme when introduced to India resulted in the assassination of its champion. Instead of sterilisation Michell offered the biblical exhortation "Be fruitful and multiply". Michell's counter proposition, that population was really declining, was buttressed by arguments taken from Cobbett. This great individualist was enlisted as a prime Radical Traditionalist. He had warned against the worship of Commerce and this echoed the theme of Radical Traditionalist Papers No.1 that a new monstrous growth (Cobbett's *The Thing*) was devouring everything, people and lands.

This idea of deterioration instead of improvement had been central in *The Flying Saucer Vision*. There had been a high point or quantum leap when intelligence was given — at the beginning. *The Fanatic* had offered another stepping stone in the logic with a blow against the champion of atheistic philosophy, A.J. Ayer. *The Fanatic's* main feature had dealt with another great crank and his crazy notion. Not the usual crank such as a believer in UFOs but Darwin, one of the pillars of modern orthodoxy. A page of illustrations had given a foretaste of *Simulacra*. "Frost on the window can look like a tree ... A tree can look like a bear ... Rocks naturally aspire to anthropomorphism and tend to reproduce the features of their human neighbours ... Human faces occur throughout nature ... " The logic was remorseless. "The simian visaged Charles Darwin thought that because some people are ape-like ... "

Eventually Michell would develop a full-blown attack on Darwinism which he had published in four periodicals 1980-81. In subsequent interviews he has emphasised the importance of countering The Darwinian Myth as "one of the greatest sources of error". Why? "The ideas of Darwin seem to destroy the whole concept of human nature." Darwinism is objectional at all levels. There are so many explanations of Mankind's origin and destiny of which Darwinism is the least attractive and most inplausible. The bigoted claims made by its propagandists only compound this revulsion. At the other extreme the theory of evolution is alien to all traditional explanations. Like the metric system this novelty is seen as a source of pride by admirers.

To conclude this sequence of how Michell takes the unfashionable view, here is a combination of the wrong sexual politics with wrong thinking on Progress. Speaking of "an inhuman view of things which regards people as units to be conveniently slotted into a rationalist one-world system", Michell offered an example. "Women keep up the customs. Usually in all societies women decide who is going to be married, buried, how one is going to eat, how one is going to *everything* in society. Once there's uncertainty and standards are abolished and everything's down to innovation and inventiveness, then it's natural that traditional people — women and such — become confused and discriminated against and that's what's happened. I know women like to deny the traditionalist role of women but it seems that History demonstrates that as a fact of Nature."[9]

If there is any doubt that Michell's images have been overtaken by the market place and are bought and

sold, a glance at the magazine in which the 1985 interview appeared will help. Its cover entices with recipes for
happiness: Acupuncture and the Ear, Seven Steps to
Optimum Health, How Your Food Choices Affect the
World. This appetite for nostrums is inclusive. The
magazine carried a Pen Pal Service for prisoners, the first
being on Death Row. This column is next to ads for A
New Concept in Diapering, Macrobiotic Hotline and
"Spicy fresh green cedar needle sachets which last for
ever AND repel moths (naturally)". The back cover is
all Eden Foods.

Real life threw up another gift when the British
House of Lords debated UFOs. It would be hard to find
two more extreme examples of human idiocy. In Britain
the Lords provoke anger and awe. Or amusement that
anybody could believe in their existence. Their proceed-
ings are a standard joke on the lines that they prove
there is life after death. If one could believe in the value
of the House of Lords one could believe in the existence
of UFOs. Had the aliens brought intelligence? Here was a
priceless combination. For such a body to seriously debate such a subject offered a parody on any attempt to
prove or disprove anything by human intelligence.
Human oddities exhibited every variety of belief and dis-
belief. Michell's explanatory notes — on UFOs or the
Lords — were models of ironic detail. A further elegant,
gentlemanly touch was the space afforded the aristocrat
of UFO believers, Le Poer Trench, who it transpired was
really Lord Clancarty!

If it is possible to array arguments for and against
UFOs which showed the futility of proof and therefore
of belief, then could the same be done with other

phenomena? Would this 'prove' the idea that the universe obligingly reflects back any image projected onto it? In this Fortean, or Platonic, mood Michell returned to the stones. Megalithomania elaborated on the joke of *A Little History of Astro Archaeology*. That had dealt in a linear way with the paradox, *Megalithomania* went into multiple dimensions. It explored how a subject attracts and stimulates cranks. The effect of the sites and the Earth Spirit (like UFOs) on characters could be seen in a flash. It transformed their lives so that they had to follow their new obsession. As those who were affected by flying saucers acquired a flying saucer vision so the study of stones (megaliths) caused a similar sort of madness, megalithomania.

Was this ability to be overwhelmed to the point of lunacy dependent on UFOs, leys, stones, etc or was it an eternal part of human nature? Eccentric Lives and Peculiar Notions took Michell's enquiries away from all sorts of external triggers, or dei ex machina. The quality was inherent. I agree with Ms Schreiber that *Eccentric Lives and Peculiar Notions* marks a major turning point for Michell. More than any previous study it puts human character and belief centre stage. If *Simulacra* offered a freak show of matter, *Living Wonders* and *Inventorum Natura* a freak show of flora and fauna, *Phenomena* a freak show of psychic abilities, then *Eccentric Lives and Peculiar Notions* is a circus act which makes the humans themselves into performers. The metaphor is now itself.

In *The Speakers* (1964) Heathcote Williams had used the outpourings of unrestrained spirits at the official site of 'free speech', Speakers' Corner, as a metaphor. His achievement was likened to a rock. "Looks like part of an important discovery: documentary novel freed from Zola. Williams writes with Blake's etching tool." *Eccentric Lives and Peculiar Notions* brings Michell into the world usually monopolised by literature. Yet like the speakers, Michell's examples are real. Again his work has transcended boundaries. As his early books mixed folk lore and antiquarianism with occultism to challenge Science, now in *Eccentric Lives and Peculiar Notions* he is on the threshold of using 'documentary' to produce stories and myth. All the metaphors which he had previously used to express the essence were only images of the beast. This essence is not the monopoly of artists any more than of psychologists, mystics, scientists or madmen. It is the realm of ideas aspired to by Plato, the 'supra-celestial place' where the Ideas of all things originate. People returning from this realm of unformed essence can aspire to the ideal, conform to the ideal, or express the ideal. Or they can seize on a form in which the Idea is conveyed. Hence the fixation on outward forms or husks which are sometimes visited by inspiration.

An author whose short life (he died aged 23) was as strangely driven as Artaud's or Strindberg's was the German, Buchner. He found a metaphor in another noted eccentric, Lenz, about whom he wrote a fragment which is considered "By all standards one of the most remarkable pieces of German narrative prose ever composed". The unique shapes of style echo the peculiar twists in the story. Lenz excuses his mad behaviour as "The simplest, purest people were those who were near the elemental; that the more refined a man's feelings and

life, the more blunted this elemental sense becomes."
This deterioration in the organs of perception had led
Man from "a feeling of endless bliss . . . in such close
contact with the particular life of every form, to have a
soul for rocks, metals, water, and plants, to take into
himself, as in a dream, every element of Nature, like
flowers that breathe with the waxing and waning of the
moon." Buchner's description of his hero's inspired state
is reminiscent of other driven sensitives like the morbid
monsters of Poe or the divine criminals of Dostoyevsky.
"He was frightened of the countryside, it was so narrow
that he was afraid of bumping into everything." All
belong to a tribe which lives by instinct and who see the
world as hieroglyphics. As these beings move to a different eternal rhythm so they can only hope for the mercy
of Providence.

In the 1982 interview Michell referred to a new
project which hinted at the next form he would investi-
gate: how writers are blessed by "the library angel" who
reflects back the proofs they require at the appropriate
moment. This has a bearing on theories of coincidence
which itself is a variant on the ancient idea of Fortune.
More significantly it touches on the idea of proofs, of
projections and, above all, on the flash of inspiration or
the transmission of intelligence. As with *Eccentric Lives
and Peculiar Notions* this indicates Michell has moved
away from the external apparatus of UFOs, leys, stones,
etc to the world of creating in terms of writing, painting
and music. This is a circular move as it is the world he
inhabited in the early 1960s though, in a flash, it has
obviously always been around him, as can be seen from

his continual friendly involvement with painters such as the mystic Maxwell Armfield[10], the Ruralists, Sophie Grandval and many more. Michell has always produced his own occasional paintings and poems while friends testify to his recourse to the recorder in the middle of conversations. Backed by the resources of Thames and Hudson his books have provided an unparalled collection of visible oddities, from stones to impossible formations all over the world. With painting and music, as with writing, Michell favours images that are accessible and acceptable. This led him to criticise an exhibition of Bacon's pictures on the grounds that such intimate horrors should be reserved for initiates like pathologists or ministers.[11]

The basic elements of language, letters, had been manipulated by Number in *City of Revelation*. Their values as sounds was explored in a talk Michell gave in the early 1980s. To illustrate his case he offered rhymes of his own. These were increased to cover the alphabet for *Euphonics, a Poet's Dictionary of Sounds* soon to be published. It promises to be every bit as irritating, amusing and stimulating as *Simulacra*. The idea that the basic elements are available for manipulation means that poets and authors, by expressing eternal truths, perform a sort of magic because they change and recreate the world.

By treating human oddities in terms of character *Eccentric Lives and Peculiar Notions* freed Michell from the reformation of Science. He was able to indulge his long affection for the lesser 'hidden' glories of English Letters. Reference has been made to his admiration for Cobbett[12] and Peacock and, following publication of

*Eccentric Lives and Peculiar Notions*, he reactivated his enthusiasm for another of these English oddities, Gissing. In the early 1970s Michell had compiled The Bed-Sitting Room Anthology which contained examples of the quirkiness of the human spirit in that new kind of hermitage. This peculiar area had been investigated by writers like Dostoyevsky and Strindberg, but Gissing offered a wonderfully English variation. In a major study of Gissing, Michell would show his profound interest in the peculiarities of human nature. "Distrustful of the easy answer given by his socialist friends, that the decline in popular culture was due entirely to the oppressions of capitalism, Gissing delved into the characters of ordinary individuals. The flaws he detected in them, producing monstrous people and thus a monstrous body of society, seemed to him to be inherent in human nature. In that case it was impossible to effect any radical improvement in the quality of people's lives by mere social reforms."[13] For Christmas 1983 Michell had sent as his greeting a privately produced booklet The Pallinghurst Barrow which was a reprint of a Victorian story about house-guests who have experiences in the other world under the spell of megalithomania and intoxicants. His Christmas greeting for 1984 was a fat booklet of 3 Gissing Stories. A Gissing addict is quoted who describes reading his favourite author as "a contagion". The Gissing vision?

At the time of writing Michell is still privately publishing oddities of elegance, wit and charm, and he is still in deep trouble. Radical Traditionalist Papers No.5 offered a characteristically unpredictable solution to the troubles in Ireland: The Concordance of High Monarchists of Ireland with the subtitle 'The Pattern of the Future'. In Summer 1985 he responded to two provocations: the desecration of Stonehenge by a police riot and the persecution of the latter-day tribal folk — a sorry echo of the great nation of the psychedelic age. As this essay goes to press (Summer '86) Michell has revised Radical Traditionalist Papers No.6 with a more accusative title designed to resolve the crisis still looming over Stonehenge and hence society.

By the mid 1980s, was England any different from the time when Michell's ideas had been formed? Reaction against everything symbolised by The Sixties had produced a nostalgia for the clampdown minds of the 1950s, amongst trendsetters and the government. A low version of 'the perennial philosophy' emerged as Thatcher's gospel of eternal values. Really these were the values introduced by the Industrial Revolution and which were exposed by Cobbett as The Thing[14]. Nevertheless — then as now. Michell's transformed version of *City of Revelation*, now The Dimensions of Paradise, promises ever more visible signs in the form of new diagrams of harmonies. Michell is still creating celestial cities which shimmer above and around us eternally.

As shown, Michell's work was a cause of the breakout rather than the result. During the 1970s he still had to fight against orthodoxies which declared him heretical. His work can be seen as a symbol of the eternal struggle of the human spirit to be free, whether from the ice-age of the pre-Sixties or of the Eighties. It proves that, like toads imprisoned in rock, a metamorphosis is possible. A great leap in intelligence will come in a flash and transform all living creatures.

# FOOTNOTES

1. *Quicksilver Messenger;* Interview Part I; (1982).

2. *The Flying Saucer Vision;* Conclusion.

3. Published in *Albion* magazine as 'UFOs and the Message from the Past'; (May 1968).

4. *Some Observations on the Discovery of Numbers;* Ealing First Year Graphics; (1968).

5. Findhorn anthology; (1969).

6. *Getting Back Together;* Robert Houriet; Abacus (1975); US edition (1969).

7. *The New View Over Atlantis;* Preface; (1984).

8. *Footprint* magazine published by Americans for Customary Weight and Measure.

9. *Quicksilver Messenger;* Interview Part II; (1982).

10. *Dynamic Symmetry in the work of Maxwell Armfield;* Michell's essay in the catalogue for Armfield's exhibition (1978).

11. Essay in *Temenos;* (July 1986).

12. Essay on Cobbett's 'Cottage Economy'; *New Seed;* (1976).

13. *Grumbling,* review of new Gissing studies *Spectator*; (July 1983); For Christmas 1986 Michell and AdCo published another Gissing story: 'An Artist at Glastonbury'.

14. References to Cobbetts *The Thing; op.cit.* pp59, 76.

*On the following pages are advertisements for concerns which have been associated with John Michell and which have kindly made possible this celebratory book.*

If you have enjoyed
AN ENGLISH FIGURE
may we invite you to peep into the
weird world of
BOZO
and hunt further for the
spirit of England . . .
50p secures our lists

BOZO
BM BOZO
LONDON WC1N 3XX
ENGLAND

# John Michell
publisher of:

**THE RADICAL TRADITIONALIST PAPERS**
 1. A Defence of Sacred Measures
 2. A Defence of People and Population
 3. The Fall of Babylon
 4. To Represent Our Saviour as "that great cock"
 5. The Concordance of High Monarchists of Ireland
 6. Stonehenge (second edition, revised)
 7. Shakespeare (due Spring 1987)
 Also: The Propaganda of the Metric System

**WEST COUNTRY EDITIONS**
 Bladud of Bath

**POCKET PALS SERIES**
 Three Stories by George Gissing
 Lost Lyonesse
 A Victim of Circumstance

*11 Powis Gardens, London W11, England*
write for lists and further information

Stonehenge, Yesterday — Looking South East.

**BOOKS BY JOHN MICHELL**
from
**THAMES & HUDSON LIMITED**
**30 Bloomsbury Street, London WC1**

The Earth Spirit
Its Ways, Shrines and Mysteries

A Little History of Astro-Archaeology

Phenomena — A Book of Wonders

Simulacra
with 196 illustrations of Faces and Figures
in Nature

Megalithomania

Living Wonders
Mysteries and Curiosities of the Animal World

The New View Over Atlantis

Eccentric Lives and Peculiar Notions

The Dimensions of Paradise